BOOK
of
SLOTH
PHILOSOPHY

How to live your
best sloth life

Jennifer McCartney

HarperCollins*Publishers*

Contents

Part One
A Sloth Education

Part Two
A Practical Guide

I've stopped trying and it feels so good.

Part One
A Sloth Education

Introduction: Welcome to the Sloth Philosophy

Slow down. Hold your horses. Chill out. Don't run on the pool deck. We're constantly being encouraged to embrace stillness. Slowness. Mindfulness. And with good reason. Science has proven that slowing down has loads of advantages – from helping to manage chronic pain to increasing happiness levels and decreasing feelings of stress.

Yet we're often shamed when we take time for ourselves. Appearing lazy is a cardinal sin in our highly strung society. (It's also one of the seven deadly sins. If that's an issue, this book is definitely not for you.) God forbid you lie on a couch once in a while with a pile of chips and cheese, rather than cooking a perfectly balanced meal from scratch using eggs and mustard and whatever else might be in your fridge … *Go do something! Make the bed! Book a holiday! Answer those texts! Feed your children!* And so we do. And because of this our lives often seem to be chaotic and short of time.

We live in a world where people jog for fun. Where a meditation app has to remind you to breathe deeply. Where you can buy a shrink-wrapped, pre-peeled orange (*No time to peel! I'm busy!*). Which is why abandoning our hang-ups about laziness and *taking it slow* is more important now than ever before. Slowing down provides us with a ton of benefits. It's time to reclaim laziness, take back our time and protest the rat race by staying in bed. And what better mascot for the take-it-slow movement than the incredible, adorable sloth.

Long-limbed, two- or three-toed, a little bit shaggy and a lot wide-eyed, the sloth is one of the cutest (and laziest) animals on the planet. These Amazon dwellers are not only essential to Central and South America's rainforests, they also have a lot to teach us about the way we live life.

Sloths are mindfulness in action. They're contemplative, deliberate, relaxed and focused. They aren't concerned with politics, or who drank the last of the milk, or how many steps they logged on their fitness tracker. They don't really stress about anything. *Live slow, die whenever* is their motto. They're wonderful animals. They resist the urge to be productive and the social pressure to be more successful. They've also been on this planet for tens of millions of years – a testament to the wisdom of their way of life, no? They must be doing something right. And now you, too, can live slothfully by embracing the sloth philosophy. It's a simple mindset and a wonderful way of life – and it doesn't take much to begin living the way of the sloth. In fact, you'll be pleased to learn, it takes very little effort. Which is a key part of the sloth philosophy.

So don't rush. And get ready to relax and unwind. Got a blanket handy? Some flannel pyjamas? Maybe a mug of tea?* Good. Now read on. And soak up the take-it-slow wisdom of the sloth.

---

* Please note the sloth philosophy embraces the best/least ridiculous parts of hygge, while dispensing with all the candles and socks. This isn't just about taking time out to have a biscuit. Plus 'sloth' is easier to pronounce.

I've been reading this book for four years
and I couldn't be happier about it.

Follow the SLOW Method for a More Slothful Life

The mantra of the sloth philosophy is slow down. To help ease yourself into this world, try following the SLOW method, outlined here. These four simple tips will help you become the best, most slothful version of yourself.

S

Sleep in. The world has a bizarre obsession with policing the amount of sleep we all get. On the one hand, we are being told how important it is, but on the other, being sleep deprived is sometimes even seen as a badge of honour. *Oh, she runs her own company and only needs four hours of sleep a night. Let's* *give her an award that she's too exhausted to enjoy!* But what if you sleep for, say, 12 hours? It's too much. You'll get some sort of laziness disease. Why fetishise sleeping in? Just do it. Sleep is good for you. Dreaming is good for you. It's great for your skin and your immune system – and your emails can wait another hour or two while you pay homage to the duvet gods.

L

Leave your phone at home. This may seem obvious, but the idea of leaving your phone at home may also give you an anxiety attack. *How will you find your way to the nearest Starbucks without your GPS?* Trust me, you'll find one. We're all too plugged in. Too much screen time is ruining our brains and expanding our waistlines. Not looking at your phone every four minutes is better for you. But it's also really hard to do. So to start, try leaving your phone at home the next time you pop out to the shops or run across the street for a flat white. See how it feels to be without your pocket technology for five minutes. Ten minutes. And over a period of days or weeks, work your way up to a couple of hours. The notifications can wait until you get back – and for those few minutes or hours take a deep breath and enjoy not being 100 per cent available and on call to the entire universe. If you can't bear to leave your phone at home, try putting it on flight mode. You know, like you're supposed to do on aeroplanes before they take off, so your Wi-Fi doesn't bring down the plane.

O

Opt out. Embracing the way of the sloth requires an attitude adjustment. Make a choice to opt out of the idea that you need to be busy, engaged, connected and productive at all times. It's just fine to be unpro-ductive every so often. In fact, the sloth philosophy believes it's essential to good mental health. Opting out on a practical level simply means doing less of the things you don't want to do. Life comes with a lot of obligations, sure, and some of them are necessary for your own wellbeing or that of your loved ones. This includes things like feeding the cat or paying your rent. But we also commit to a lot of things we don't necessarily want or need to do. Part of slowing down and embracing the sloth philosophy is realising you don't have to do everything or be all things to everyone. Being busy isn't a badge of honour if you're miserable.

'What's the rush?' Repeat this phrase when you're feeling overwhelmed or stressed out. Ask yourself whether something really needs doing immediately. Are you ignoring your own needs in order to do it? If you are about to take a rejuvenating walk in the spring sunshine, but get a text message from your accountant asking about a missing file which causes you to check your email where you see a note from a friend asking about your plans for visiting the countryside tomorrow which you start to reply to but first you need to research that art gallery you heard about so you can include the link in your reply and then it's an hour later and somehow you've bought four pair of shoes from ASOS (also that reminds you that before your trip you need to wash your sneakers, throw out the rotten fridge lettuce and call the school) … you need to rethink your priorities. Take a step back. Try and put any feelings of urgency into perspective. Remember our collective past when our grandparents sent paper letters to their friends and family via boats? Catching up with each other took weeks. And they all survived. Take a breath. Vow to do it later. Or tomorrow. If at all. Will anyone or anything suffer if you take that walk first?

Quiz

What's Your Sloth Personality?

Your ideal book is:

A. fun and entertaining; preferably with pictures; maybe some manga

B. the latest in fine literature; probably Zadie Smith or Ali Smith

C. preferably about astrology, and definitely an audio book (Who has the energy to actually hold a book these days?)

D. a rush-to-publication memoir – by someone who's been famous for fewer than eight months

E. something inspiring like *How to Live Hard, Hustle Hard and Love Your Life to the Fullest*

When your boss tells you something needs to be done urgently you:

A. give her a thumbs-up and resolve to get to it after lunch; tomorrow after lunch, probably

B. silently contemplate the best way to get the thing done

C. take a nap

D. get some snacks and then watch a video online about how best to do the thing

E. clear your schedule, open a spreadsheet and wait for the waves of anxiety

Quiz

When it comes to snacking you reach for:

A. cheese-flavoured snacks

B. green tea and sushi

C. cereal with marshmallows

D. a bottle of meal-replacement liquid

E. diet water

If you could sum up your outlook on life with a trite phrase, it would be:

A. it's 4:20 somewhere

B. silence isn't empty; it's full of answers

C. sleep, perchance to dream

D. hide your wife, hide your kids

E. work hard, hustle harder

Laying in the sun since 1981.

Answers

Mostly As: stoner sloth. Not much bothers you. You like to eat your leaves and chill in peace. Friends love you for your zero-drama, laid-back approach to the world.

Mostly Bs: meditative sloth. You're an independent, introspective sloth. You like beaches, being a Libra or Scorpio, and taking time to paint your nails and read a book. It's intellectual stimulation, solitude and self-care that you crave.

Mostly Cs: sloth goddess Aergia. Some people are energetic, practical, get-up-and-go types. And others, like you, are dreamers – just living for your next nap. You know that getting a full twelve hours is the best way to recharge. Like the goddess of sloth, Aergia, you live for being lazy.

Mostly Ds: 'Let-me-tell-you-about-the-latest-sloth-meme' sloth. In front of the computer* is your personal sloth style and you've had at least one social-media post go viral. You love popular culture, keeping up with the latest memes, experimenting with up-to-the-minute trends and kicking back with your feet up. Friends love you as you're always effortlessly informed about everything.

Mostly Es: manic sloth. You're less of a sloth and more of a cheetah. Remember the SLOW method and try and relax a little bit – too much running around can be bad for your health. In fact, if sloths move too quickly they can die from expending too much energy. Let that be a warning.

---

*   But not at a standing or treadmill desk. Your screen time is strictly sitting-down time.

Welcome to my book pile, this should last a lifetime.

Famous Followers of the Sloth Philosophy

The sloth philosophy has its own heroes – men and women who get up late, procrastinate, take lots of breaks and (surprise) manage to get stuff done in their own time. Because of their fame and success, you may not associate them with a sloth lifestyle. But rest assured, if you rest first, you'll probably get around to it eventually – just like the winners you'll read about here.

DOUGLAS ADAMS

Douglas Adams came up with the idea for the title of *The Hitchhiker's Guide to the Galaxy* while lying drunk in a field – not the first time being drunk or taking a nap has paid off, so let this be a lesson to us all. He was also notoriously bad with deadlines, saying, 'I love deadlines. I love the whooshing noise they make as they go by.' The author's book editor reportedly once spent three weeks locked in a hotel room with him to ensure he wrote and delivered the manuscript for *So Long, and Thanks for All the Fish*. He even recalls doing very little work at university – completing three essays in as many years. He graduated nonetheless, and went on to become one of England's most successful and best-known authors – all at his own pace.

LEONARDO DA VINCI

Guess how long it took famous sloth-philosophy hero da Vinci to finish the *Mona Lisa*? (Keep in mind the painting is only 21 by 30 inches.) A year? Three years? Scholars think it could have taken as many as fifteen. For the purposes of comparison, keener Michelangelo took just four years to paint the entire Sistine Chapel. Today, few of us care how long it took anyone from history to do anything – all that matters is that eventually, when they felt like it, they did it. Da Vinci also took 25 years to complete a seven-month commission – his first payment for *Virgin of the Rocks* being received in 1483 and the final one in

1508. And what was he doing with all that down-time? Doodling. Inventing the helicopter and the parachute and the tank.

LORD MELBOURNE
Lord Melbourne was by all accounts an unexceptional English prime minister. He didn't oversee any wars or enact any notable policies. He's mostly remembered for his extramarital affairs while in office and for his close relationship with Queen Victoria. Doing nothing was his default position. 'Why not leave it alone?' was his mantra (along with the words 'delay' and 'postpone'). He was a man who served in his job adequately – we can all aspire to that.

FRANK LLOYD WRIGHT
In a situation that may be familiar to any sloth-philosophy adherent (and one that will strike fear into those conditioned to believe everything should always be done well in advance with months of preparation), witness Frank Lloyd Wright's last-minute scramble to show he'd been working on a commission he'd actually ignored. According to his

apprentices, Wright received an unexpected call from his patron, Edgar Kaufmann Sr, who mentioned he was in the neighbourhood and wanted to stop by to see the plans for his new house, Fallingwater. Wright had told the businessman that he'd been working on it when he'd done absolutely nothing since their original meeting nine months earlier. In the two hours it took Kaufmann to drive to see Wright, the architect quickly drew up plans for the now world-famous design. A lesson to all of us that what looks like laziness is often just the most efficient way of doing things. Why spend nine months working on something that can be done in two hours?

EDITH WHARTON

The famous American author of *House of Mirth* liked to write in bed. (Perhaps if we all had an estate in Massachusetts, we might be inclined to do the same.) Her friend Gaillard Lapsley described a typical day for the author: 'She would have her writing board perilously furnished with an ink-pot on her knee, the dog of the moment under her left elbow and the bed strewn with correspondence, newspapers and books.'

Dogs, books and a bed. Sounds perfectly reasonable, doesn't it? No grey cubicles or fancy desk chairs needed to get proper work done. In fact, the Edith Wharton Restoration organisation has restored the author's luxury bedroom suite (bedroom, boudoir and bath) where she wrote, so you can go see for yourself and be inspired.

COLETTE

Colette was in her thirties and felt like a failure, her writing career not yet having taken off. (In a world of over-achieving 17-year-olds it was only too easy to feel like you'd aged out and missed your chance at fame.) Nevertheless, she persisted, with the help of a very strict writing routine: Colette would only begin to write after she'd groomed her French bulldog. Sounds reasonable.

'To write is the joy and the torment of the idle,' she said.

If I had opposable thumbs I'd be making the 'om' sign.

Part Two
A Practical Guide

Health and Wellness

*In a world of extreme sports, 85-hour work weeks
and fast food, the sloth philosophy of health and
wellness can help you slow down, relax and
regain your equilibrium.*

Sloth Philosophy
Slow down for better health

'For fast-acting relief, try slowing down.'

Lily Tomlin

Sloth Fact: Sloths are the slowest mammals on earth. On the ground their top speed is about 4 metres per minute. In an emergency (*must use the toilet in the next four or five days!*) they can do about 4.5 metres per minute.

Sneaker companies, fitness bloggers and the Olympics want us to believe that extreme sports and intense physical exercise are admirable endeavours. That's because high-intensity workouts with lots of cardio have become synonymous with discipline and dedication, in addition to being necessary for our general health and wellbeing. *Forget moderation and just run a marathon or do fifty crunches a day or climb Mount Kilimanjaro* – this is the path to wellness and longevity we're encouraged to pursue. God help anyone born with bad ankles or an inner-ear issue.

But now the sloth philosophy is here to let you know that working out is for chumps. Or, to put it more mildly, there's more than one way to stay healthy and it doesn't involve pooping yourself while running an 18-hour ultra-marathon. Scientists are now learning what sloths already know: moving slowly has its benefits. That's right. Activities like yoga and tai chi (also known as slow-movement therapy) have been proven to reduce chronic pain. Practitioners of these chill workout routines even report taking fewer opiates. And a 2008 study conducted at Tufts Medical Center in Boston found that 12 weeks of tai chi helped reduce pain and stress levels in arthritis patients. One theory about why these low-impact exercises work so well is that the slow movement increases our relaxation response. This, in turn, reduces our stress response and boosts our immune function. Even a brisk walk can be beneficial – and it's much easier on the knees than running.

No matter what kind of slow exercises you choose to do, slow, rhythmic breathing and controlled movements are key. Remind you of anything? Right, sloths. So remember that there's more than one way to get into shape and improve your health.

Sloth Philosophy
Breathe deeply – even if you're upside down

> **Sloth Fact:** A sloth's internal organs are fixed in place, to keep their weight away from the diaphragm and avoid crushing its lungs. This allows it to breathe easily in any position – an evolutionary necessity, given that the sloth's favoured position is upside down.

Breathing properly should be an easy thing to do. Our lives depend on it. *I'm breathing right now,* you might think. *What's the big deal?* The problem is, we're often not breathing effectively, and this can negatively impact our health. We're so tense, or hunched over, or distracted that we're barely taking in or exhaling more than a little puff of air. Computers

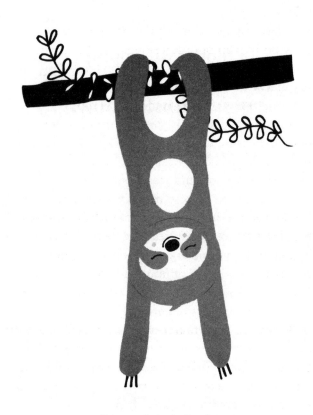

Standing upright is for chumps.
Embrace the upside down.

and stress are the main culprits. Bad posture as we tap away on our laptops means our ribs are digging into our diaphragms, so our lungs don't have room to expand. Stress can make our breath short and shallow – a condition known as underbreathing.

Breathing deeply is an important practice to develop because it can reduce stress and lower blood pressure. It promotes healing by increasing oxygen levels in the blood and it's even thought to reduce inflammation. A 2016 study at the Medical University of South Carolina found that just 20 minutes of breathing exercises resulted in a decrease in salivary cytokines – a biomarker for inflammation. That means a few minutes of mindful breathing can actually benefit our bodies on a molecular level. And because the wonders of better breathing are scientifically proven, you'll find these techniques practised by everyone from yogis to military personnel to athletes. So straighten up. Set your shoulders back. Give those lungs room to expand. And take a deep breath. Take two. Keep it up. Feels good, right?

I'd count the stars if I weren't so lazy.
Best to just look and enjoy.

Sloth Philosophy
Seek the quiet place

Sloth Fact: Sloths have teeny, tiny ears and can't hear very well. Most of their life is spent in relative silence. Ah, bliss ...

Noise pollution can be harmful to our physical and mental health, but, unlike sloths, we can't retreat to the treetops whenever we feel overwhelmed. Prolonged exposure to loud noise can cause hearing loss, sleep disturbances, high blood pressure and increased stress levels. The World Health Organization recommends decibel levels of no more than 50 in residential areas, but that's wishful thinking for a large portion of the population. (To put that in context, sirens are 120 decibels, while construction noise can measure between 80 and 90 and the noise from a passing subway train is about 80.) Our cities have become so loud that scientists have discovered that robins are now singing at night rather than during the day. Whatever the birds have to communicate (news of another royal birth?) it can't be done during the day in our major cities. Not surprisingly, perhaps, 8 of the UK's top 10 districts ranked by noise complaints per 1,000 residents are in London. Londoners do love a good knees-up. And New York City is no better, with hundreds of thousands of noise complaints lodged every year. Not for nothing is it known as the city that never sleeps!

While most of us can't help where we live, we can take steps to mitigate the noise pollution we experience. So unless you're planning to pick up and move to an off-the-grid tiny house in the wilderness sometime soon, here are some common-sense ways to increase the level of peace and quiet in your life:

Out and about:
- Wear earplugs or noise-cancelling headphones.
- Avoid busy construction sites, loud parties and subways; take a walk in the park instead – see what the foxes are up to.

At home:
- Consider sound-proofing windows if you're on a busy street.
- Invest in a white-noise machine (or download a white-noise app).
- Send your children to boarding school.*
- Trade the yappy dog for a quiet cat.†
- Take a mini break somewhere off the grid.

Respite may be on the way for city dwellers, thanks to better urban planning that's looking to replace roads with bike paths or light rail and to invest in quieter trains and subways. But until then – stop,

---

* This is a joke but doing it *would* increase your peace-and-quiet levels. So … up to you.
† Ditto.

listen and be aware of your surroundings when you can. And if the hum and buzz of daily life are too much, find a quiet place to escape for a while. Take a nap while you're at it.

> Slow sloth. So slow, sloth.
> Languid tree-hanging sleeper.
> Every day, Friday.

Sloth Philosophy
Don't let the haters get you down

The French naturalist Georges Buffon was the first to describe sloths in his 1749 encyclopaedia of life sciences: 'Slowness, habitual pain, and stupidity are the results of this strange and bungled conformation,' he wrote, rather rudely. 'These sloths are the lowest form of existence. One more defect would have made their lives impossible.'

Life can be tough sometimes – whether you're sloth or human, people can be judgemental about your looks, your lifestyle, your perceived 'defects'. They might say mean or petty shit that negatively impacts your mental health. If you're online, a lot of comments can even be cruel. And we're often our own worst critic: you might feel that no one believes in you, that you're all wrong for the job, that you've made a mess of things or that you're not worthy of love.

'I don't condone defacing our precious rainforests
but I love you despite your mistakes.'

But sloths remain blissfully unaware that they're 'slow' or 'stupid' or that they were once considered the lowest form of existence by some scientist. If they'd taken Buffon's negative comments to heart they might have given up. *What's the point?* they'd have thought. *No one likes us. We've been designed all wrong. We're just a strange mistake.* And yet they avoided despair, escaped extinction, made it to modern times and quietly became one of the most intriguing animals on the planet. Their slowness is an asset. Their unusual anatomy is cute. They're living their slow, slothful lives the way they were always meant to.

The sloth lives its truth. It's the rest of us that changed our ways and realised its value.

And that, my friend, is the way of the sloth. Ignore the haters. Do your own thing. And eventually, if your detractors are open-minded or enlightened enough, they might even come to appreciate you.★

★   If not, bugger 'em. You're the best.

Whether it's your BFF or a tree,
sometimes it's just nice to hug something.

Sloth Philosophy
Trees are your friends: embrace forest bathing

Sloth Fact: Sloths spend most of their time in trees. They really prefer nature to people. And that's part of the reason they're so relaxed, probably.

There's a cool wellness trend you may have read about called forest bathing (don't worry, prudes – you can forest bathe with your clothes on). Popularised in Japan, where it's been an important part of preventative medicine since the 1980s, *shinrin-yoku* means 'forest bathing' or 'taking in the forest atmosphere'. Spending time in nature – literally looking at trees – is scientifically proven to reduce blood pressure and stress levels as well as improve sleep quality, mood, energy levels and focus. Sloths already know this, of course – that's why they're so stress-free. So go find a forest and stand in it. Even a little park will do. Breathe in and out, look around and go ahead – give a tree a hug. You'll feel better.

A patch of grass will also work. And if you can't get out at all, try stocking up on some house plants. They can improve productivity and concentration levels by up to 15 per cent, while also reducing stress and boosting your mood.

Sloth Philosophy
The Sloth Philosophy of Sports

'I don't think necessity is the mother of invention. Invention, in my opinion, arises directly from idleness, possibly also from laziness – to save oneself trouble.'

Agatha Christie

We're going to skip over American football even though it is the slowest-moving sport ever imagined when you really think about it. There are three seconds of action for every 15 minutes they stand around discussing plays. We all know it puts you at risk for concussions and then brain damage. So instead, let's look at other sporting endeavours that embrace the philosophy of the sloth without injuring you in the process.

By the time the sloths climbed up to their
respective podiums it was morning and
the crowds had gone home.

CURLING

This is a deceptively difficult sport to play and it plays havoc with your knees and thigh muscles. But *watching* the sport is both soothing and exciting. The stone slides gracefully down the ice behind the manic, brushy people smoothing its way. It's a sport that requires dignity and teamwork. Plus it's easy to follow.

SHUFFLEBOARD

This genteel sport is similar to curling except it's played at a much slower pace and with lighter equipment. Using a stick, players shove a small weighted disc along the court with the goal of sliding it into the scoring triangle. The team with the highest number of points wins. Because of the minimal physical requirements, it's a game often associated with the elderly – but because everyone who's anyone is lazy now, it's recently become popular with hipsters, too.

DARTS

This game embraces the sloth philosophy, as the sport (at its lower levels) basically revolves around drinking and having fun with your friends while occasionally exerting your arm and eye muscles just enough to throw a dart in the direction of a wall. Often, there's a sweet spot with darts where you've had enough beer to become very excellent at it before the downward slide where you begin throwing the dart at the table or floor.

SWIMMING

More specifically, hot-tubbing. A study from the UK's Loughborough University found that sitting in a hot tub for an hour burned about 140 calories. It also slightly lowered participants' blood-sugar levels. So enjoy the sauna, the hot tub and the bubble bath at every opportunity. Because passive is where it's at. Or do some leisurely laps – after all, the sloth philosophy is all about taking it easy in a way that feels right for you.

CROQUET

Yes, it is a sport, I looked it up. And a more genteel and slow-moving sport you'd be hard pressed to find. It originated in England or possibly France (the sloth philosophy is all about not being bothered by details like this) and involves thwacking a heavy ball through a hoop with a mallet. Manet painted a bunch of people playing croquet, as did Norman Rockwell and Winslow Homer. The point being that the game is played so slowly that artists were able to paint it.

BOCCE

Bocce is like bowling, but instead of rolling a ball down a slick wooden lane, you bowl over dirt. So this is a great sport for anyone that finds regular bowling too fast paced. The idea is that you throw a little ball onto a court and then throw four other balls as close as you can to the initial one. The team with the most balls closest to the little ball wins. There's a lot of standing around involved in bocce, which gives you time to drink and chat, that being the best part of sports anyway. When people have the opportunity to drink they'll play any sort of game, no matter how weird, and bocce fits the bill.

Quiz

Which Sloth Sport is Best for Your Personality?

When you imagine a really enjoyable day of sportsmanship, you're picturing:

A. a TV

B. a long road ahead and people on the sidelines cheering you on

C. horses, hats and a few of your old chums from Eton

D. a good fair match between two talented people or teams

What's your ideal sports drink?

A. Pint of beer

B. Blue Power Vitamin Water with B12

C. Champagne

D. Water with lemon

The best kit consists of:

A. denim and a polo shirt

B. breathable fabrics with air-wick technology

C. a linen suit

D. all-white everything

Answers

Mostly As: darts. You're a legend down at your local. Jacob, Will and the rest of the guys still talk about the day you fell asleep trying to demonstrate a one-armed push-up on top of the bar.

Mostly Bs: 800-metre dash. You've got a lot of energy. Sloth sports are probably not for you, but your knees will pay for all your activity when you're older.

Mostly Cs: croquet. You're slothful in a high-society kind of way. You don't need to do a lot or move quickly because you pay people to do it for you.

Mostly Ds: tennis. A great sport for people who don't like sports.

Inner-tubing is popular with sloths, although
their sharp claws can pose a problem.

The happiest anyone's ever been eating a salad.

Food and Drink

How to enjoy a sushi roll these days when it might contain mercury or lead or plastics? What if I'm not making my own organic baby food? And how much wine is too much wine? The sloth philosophy of food is all about chilling the hell out and consuming whatever you want.

Sloth Philosophy
Eat slowly

'The quest for slowness, which begins as a simple rebellion against the impoverishment of taste in our lives, makes it possible to rediscover taste.'

Carlo Petrini, founder of the
International Slow Food Movement

Sloth Fact: It can take up to a month for a sloth to digest a meal. Talk about slow food! They have the slowest metabolism in the animal kingdom.

While we cannot help how quickly we digest our food we can make an effort to *consume* it more slowly and with more joy. Sloths have a lot in common with the Slow Food Movement which started in Italy in the 1980s as an antidote to fast food. It advocates eating fresh, locally produced food, preferably around a table with friends and family – the kind of meal with six courses, numerous bottles of wine, perhaps eaten at a table overlooking the Mediterranean in the sunshine, followed by grappa and espresso; the kind of meal that takes nine hours to enjoy. Heaven. Of course, we all eat fast food and takeaways sometimes because they're convenient. And there's no shame in that. So the sloth philosophy of slow eating is all about mindful eating, even if it's not expensive locally sourced organic produce that you bought from a farmer an hour ago. It's about savouring whatever it is you choose to eat wherever you choose to eat it – whether it's a pastry on the train or a ham sandwich on a park bench. (If you're feeling guilty about what you're eating, that's missing the point.)

If you really want to go full on with this one, though, take a tip from the sloth and the next time it's sunny out, go have a picnic. There's no better manifestation of the Slow Food Movement (sloth-philosophy style) than eating and drinking on a blanket in the sun with friends. Get some cheese, bread, wine and grapes. Or a sausage roll and a Scotch egg – whatever floats your boat. Then eat it all slowly, nibbling away over the course of an hour or two. Relax. Taking time to be mindful and enjoy what you're consuming means you're bringing yourself pleasure. Maybe you're also supporting local farmers (or your local Indian takeaway). Maybe you're eating healthy, fresh food (or maybe your next meal will be healthier, whatever). Whatever's in your maw at the moment, enjoy it. That's the slow food movement, sloth style.

Sloth Philosophy
Better living with bok choy

*'Offer the lazy an egg, and they'll
want you to peel it for them.'*

Lithuanian proverb

Sloth Fact: Sloths are predominantly herbivores and
eat mostly leaves, twigs and fruits. Their favourite
tree to nibble on is the quick-growing cecropia which
is found in the rainforests of South America.

Adding a few more leafy greens to your diet may
seem obvious (*Yes, Mum, I know this sausage roll
and ginger beer aren't part of a balanced meal*). But knowing what's good for you and making healthy choices

This is the one that gets you high, right?

are two different things. The sloth philosophy isn't about being evangelical, of course. Whether you're a meat-and-potatoes person or you're dabbling with vegetarianism, the sloth philosophy is simply about remembering to eat a few greens a little more often. But how to eat better when that head of lettuce is now a brown bog in the back of your fridge?

Luckily, capitalism is here to help – there's probably a juice bar selling cannabis cucumber smoothies around the corner from wherever you're reading this (if you're reading this in California). But seriously, the shops are full of easy ways to help you get more veg in your diet. Opt for a hummus sandwich next time instead of ham. Or choose roasted broccoli instead of potatoes for your supper. Whatever your solution, eating green will have a positive impact on your health. Leafy plants are packed with nutrients like vitamins C and K, folate, potassium and iron. One of the most important and scientifically proven benefits of eating more veg includes protection against many diseases, as well as improved digestive function, stronger bones and who knows what else? So be kind to your body and embrace the sloth philosophy of, well, eating leaves.

Sloth Philosophy
Say no to the sad desk salad

Sloth Fact: Sloths eat outside, far away from their sloth computers.*

Once you've made up your mind to have a bit of salad for lunch a few times a week, the next step is to avoid eating it at your desk. There are a number of reasons for this. To name a few, sunshine is good for you, hunching over your desk all day is bad for your posture, taking a walk is never a bad idea and making eye contact with another human is good for the soul.

---

* Sloth computers run extremely slowly, as you can imagine, so the upside to that is that sloths aren't addicted to the internet like we are and they get out a lot more.

Taking a proper lunch break also helps you to appear less sad to your co-workers.

The point is that a more slothful life requires a multi-pronged approach. I ate a sad desk salad every lunch hour for eight years and it didn't make me happier or healthier. (If I'd eaten my salad in the park and then quit my job, *that* would have been the healthy choice.) So remember that checking your work email while downing a poke bowl with zucchini noodles isn't what healthy eating is all about. Take your leaf meal outside. Sit on a bench. Sit in the park. Sit on some public steps somewhere. Sit in a café. Use your lunch break for its intended purpose. A break for lunch.

Slocktail for the lazy bartender

A real sloth cocktail begins with a traditional Costa Rican liquor – a bottle of guaro. Guaro is a clear, sweet liquor made from sugar cane. It's also very potent, so you've been warned.

INGREDIENTS
lime wedges

2 teaspoons sugar

ice

60ml (2fl oz) guaro

splash club soda

METHOD
Mash the lime wedges and sugar into a smushy mess at the bottom of your glass. Add some ice, the guaro and club soda. Stir and enjoy! It tastes like being in a hammock under the hot sun with your favourite sloth.

Sloth Philosophy
Indulge and enjoy it

Sloth Fact: The contents of a sloth's stomach can account for a huge proportion of its body mass.

S loths slowly stuff themselves on so many leaves that more than a quarter of their body weight can be attributed to undigested food. Sloths are unconcerned with this post-meal bloat, however, because they're sloths and they're just doing what comes naturally. There's no one to tell them they're overeating, that they should diversify their diet or do a cleanse.

The world is full of this kind of wellness advice that seems designed to make us feel out of control about our eating habits. *Warm water with lemon in the morning, then one garlic bulb a day for three days, followed by steamed chicken breasts and beets for the rest of the week.*

Follow this up with a coffee enema and you'll be in the clear. It's complicated and exhausting – not to mention expensive. The sloth philosophy is all about forgetting the numbers, weights, calories, kilojoules, cleanses and even the latest thinking about which superfood will keep you alive the longest. (Much of the food science we hear is conflicting. Is soy milk healthy or is oat milk better? Is red wine still OK in moderation or are we supposed to drink the whole bottle now? What about coffee? And eating pasta before bed helps you *lose* weight, you say?) The fact is, unless you're chewing on lead pipes or a box of doughnuts for breakfast, your eating habits are probably just fine.

It's easy to get caught up in the minutiae and to forget the bigger picture: we're all lucky to have enough to eat with better access to healthy, safely prepared food filled with vitamins than any other generation before us. The sloth philosophy asks that you trust yourself and your body. It's about eating or drinking what you want until you feel full or satisfied. Fuel your body with food when you feel hungry. Eat. Digest. Repeat when you feel like it. The miracle of nature!

After your morning coffee is a great time for a nap.
Actually, it's always a great time for a nap.

Quiz

What's Your Ideal Sloth Meal?

What's your favourite cooking appliance?

A. Your mobile. So you can call for a takeaway

B. Microwave

C. Garlic press

D. Your free-standing Viking oven with a dual range

If you were a breed of dog you'd be:

A. a cat

B. a rescue mutt from the local animal shelter

C. a golden retriever

D. a corgi

You've booked your next mini-break. You're heading to:

A. Goa for some beach time, then Mumbai for a bit of culture

B. Bruges for some beer and architecture

C. Marseille for some hand-milled soap and a bit of bouillabaisse

D. the Scottish Highlands for some falconing

Answers

Mostly As: curried-chicken takeaway with a glass of Sangiovese. You enjoy rich, complex flavours to be savoured that don't require a lot of effort to prepare besides ordering the food and opening the wine. Simple and elegant – that's you.

Mostly Bs: sausage roll and a vodka shot. You enjoy tasty, straightforward food without the frills. Easy to make and easy to eat, this meal is perfect for your laid-back, easy-going personality.

Mostly Cs: homemade pesto gnocchi and a G&T. Cooking is an enjoyable pastime for you, but it's not anything you get worked up about. Fresh, classic and homemade meals are your favourites. Also, gin and tonics are what sloths would drink if they were into drinking.

Mostly Ds: pheasant and a glass of Champagne. Food is something to be enjoyed slowly and savoured for as long as possible – you love the rituals that come with eating and drinking fine food. You've been known to stretch a late lunch into an early dinner and polish off a few bottles of bubbly in the process.

Know Your Sloth History

Give thanks to the sloth goddess Aergia

Sloth Fact: Sloths, although generally considered to be agnostic, do have their own goddess.

We all need someone to look up to and draw strength from now and then. A higher power of some kind. But the sloth philosophy rejects the gods of capitalism, stress and speed. (The stock exchange, email and marathoning, respectively.) We've worshipped at the altar of productivity for too long. It's time to get with a goddess that's more in line with our own image. That's why sloth followers turn to the ancient Greek goddess Aergia (which translates as 'inactivity' in Greek). The daughter of Gaia and Aither, Aergia is the goddess of laziness, idleness and sloth. She is said to guard the entrance to the cave of Hypnos – god of Sleep. Not a bad job if you can get it.

The yang to her yin is Horme, the spirit of impulse, action and effort. Today, this overachieving spark would also probably represent the spirit of hustle, #dealsinheels, and gettin' paid. Sounds like stressful capitalist bullshit, right? So embrace the goddess of sloth when you're feeling overwhelmed by emails and the sneaking feeling that you should be doing something more productive than just rewatching *The Wire* episodes while in bed with a hangover. If you need a mantra, try this: Aergia, give me the strength to do nothing.

'You look like you could use a nap' says Aergia, probably, to all those overachieving gods.

Checking off the first and only item on the to-do list.

Sleep

Sleep is a magical place where our brains go to escape from the stress of our daily lives. It's important for good health, and lots of sleep can make you feel wonderful. The sloth philosophy of sleep can help you to prioritise the Land of Nod and reject the notion that not needing a lot of sleep is somehow admirable, rather than incredibly irritating.

Sloth Philosophy
Sleep in, take a nap, then go to bed early

'How beautiful it is to do nothing, and then rest afterwards (or, Mañana, mañana).'

Spanish proverb★

Sloth Fact: Sloths sleep between 10 and 18 hours a day. They can sleep anywhere – usually upside down, clinging to a tree branch. Think about that kind of dedication next time you complain about trying to nap on an aeroplane.

★ According to the internet this is a Spanish proverb, which seems likely – based on what I understand about the Spanish lifestyle, which revolves around napping and enjoying life in the sun with wine.

Sleep

Getting a good night's rest can help boost your happiness levels and concentration, improve your short-term memory and even help you build muscle.* (Think of a famously fit person with lots of muscle and know they probably just lie around napping all day.) While you may not be a champion snoozer like the sloths (or 98 per cent of teenagers), getting enough sleep is still essential for good health. In fact, people who sleep well – those who score low on a sleep-disturbance scale – use fewer healthcare resources than those who don't. That may be because too little sleep is associated with health problems like heart disease, diabetes and obesity. So how to slothify your sleep? Chamomile tea. Whisky. Lavender oil. Fresh sheets. Melatonin. Blackout blinds. Earplugs. Sending your children to a commune somewhere … Whatever your solution, the idea is that sleep is great and productivity overrated. So stay healthy and embrace the sloth philosophy of sleep!

---

* It's strange but true. Sleeping for around 8–10 hours a night has the same effect as fasting, and this is catabolic to muscle growth.

Sloth Philosophy
Or stay up late and embrace the night

'Towards evening the lazy person begins to get busy.'★

German proverb

....
Sloth Fact: Sloths are nocturnal animals and sleep
mostly during the day.
....

Teenagers everywhere – this one's for you. The sloth philosophy believes that staying up late and sleeping in is a perfectly fine thing to do. In fact,

★ This proverb illustrates how misunderstood and maligned night owls can be in our society. Staying up late to accomplish things is just as valid as getting up early.

sleeping in is one of the key tenets of the SLOW method. But thanks to the stigma that equates a lie-in with laziness, we've been brought up to feel guilty about sleeping late. So we're not only obsessed with the idea of getting *enough* sleep, but also the idea of getting it *at the right time*. We've been conditioned to believe that 'early to bed' is ideal. Early rising is also necessary to better eat all the worms. No thanks.

The sloth philosophy is about getting enough sleep whenever and wherever you want. The fact is, just like the sloths, some of us are programmed to stay up late and sleep in thanks to differences in our chronobiology – the natural internal clock that dictates when we sleep and wake.

If you do your best work after midnight or enjoy socialising until the wee hours, you're in good company: famous night owls include Winston Churchill and Barack Obama. Oh – and another bonus? People who stay up late have statistically more sex than those who head to bed early. It's likely an evolutionary thing – being active at night means more opportunities for socialising and mating without the bother of kids or work.

I Hear the Amazon Snoring

(after 'I Hear America Singing' by Walt Whitman)

I hear sloths singing, these varied carols of
    snores I hear,
Those of two-toed sloths, each one
    singing his as it should be, lazy and
    relaxed,
The momma sloth singing hers as she
    measures the length of her nap,
The baby sloth singing his as he makes
    ready to wake then dawdle, or meander,
    or both,
The granny sloth singing what memories
    belong to her in her tree, her nurse singing
    on the forest floor,
The shaggy sloth singing as he sits on his
    branch, the shaggier son snoring as he
    snoozes,

The runaway's song (two feet from home
    since last week), the slowpoke having a
    nap in the morning, or at noon
    intermission, or at sundown,
The delicious singing of the mother, or of the
    young wife hard at work doing nothing, or
    of the girl swimming or contemplating,
Each singing what belongs to him or her and
    to none else,
The day what belongs to the day – at night
    the deep sleep of young sloths, robust,
    friendly,
Snoring in their sleep their soft melodious
    songs.

Quiz

What's Your Sloth Sleep Style?

Your evening routine consists of:

A. whisky and a novel about a murder on Capri

B. toner, serum, night cream, sleep mask

C. getting ready to go out

When it comes to pyjamas your preference is:

A. top-to-bottom flannels

B. an organic nightie from some actress's sustainable clothing line

C. none; you sleep in the buff or in whatever you were wearing when you came home at 4 am

When it comes to remembering your dreams:

A. that's what your dream journal is for

B. your sleeping pills usually knock you out so completely you don't remember your dreams

C. are they dreams? Prophecies? Who can tell? The world is magic. The stars are your children

Your ideal bedtime is:

A. whenever you fall asleep with your book

B. exactly 30 minutes after you take your pill

C. after last call at the bar

Answers

Mostly As: natural sloth sleeper. You've never had trouble getting to sleep. You love that long unwinding process right before bed that lets your mind wander and your body relax. You wake up refreshed and in tune with your body. You're a sloth sleep professional.

Mostly Bs: studious sloth sleeper. You take your sleep seriously. Being asleep is something to plan ahead and prepare for. You're not going to just conk out on any old sheets, in any old outfit, with any old person. You want a high-end, curated sleep that only the best night creams (and prescription meds) can give you. You make the sloths proud.

Mostly Cs: nocturnal nellie. Like the sloth, you're more of a nocturnal type. Sleep is to be had during the day while nighttime is for getting things done and having fun. Don't let society try to make you feel guilty about your sleep habits. They're just as valid as anyone else's.

Famous Sloths

Buttercup the Astro Sloth

Buttercup was minding her business, lounging in her hammock at the Sloth Sanctuary in Costa Rica when a bunch of internet users decided her image would make great fodder for a kind of intergalactic time capsule. A photo of Buttercup the sloth will eventually be sent to the moon on a commercial spaceship. The image of this lucky sloth, taken by photographer Pedro Dionísio, was chosen by Reddit users to be buried under the moon's south pole because sometimes the world is a bit silly.

Not working. Just banging on this drum all day.

Leisure and Pleasure

Movies, books, television and art are what make the world go around – even better, they don't require a lot of effort to enjoy. And making time to enjoy ourselves is an important part of the sloth philosophy. Can you sit still and stare at a thing? Good. Then you're ready to enjoy some art, easy listening, and take it slow literature.

Sometimes not doing something is the
greatest achievement of all.

Sloth Philosophy
Embrace the art of Slow Reading

'It is not for nothing that I have been a philologist, perhaps I am a philologist still, that is to say, a teacher of slow reading.'

Nietzsche

Sloth Fact: Did you know sloths can't read very quickly? If at all?*

I f sloths *could* read, however, they wouldn't be reading an interview with the London-based baker for Megan Markle and Prince Harry's wedding cake

★   Sloths can't read, probably. But use your imagination here.

on their phones, while also watching TV and half-listening to their spouse talking about their run-in with a rude cashier at Lidl. Sloths would read offline, carefully, while fully engaged. They'd probably underline passages they enjoy because they're thoughtful and intelligent animals.

But we're not encouraged to read slowly. We're urged to consume micro-news every other minute in order to stay informed. We learn to skim headlines, instead of reading whole articles. We're challenged to read 100 books a year and keep track of our success in this endeavour online. We're obsessed with productivity at the expense of our reading enjoyment. The careless way we read both online and off has become an epidemic, according to some worried scientists. But there is a cure: slow reading.

The Slow Book Movement advocates reading at a relaxed pace – the idea being that slow reading increases pleasure, insight and comprehension. Slow reading is about taking it all in, reading aloud, looking up words we don't know and discussing books with friends. In fact, a UK study found that just six minutes of 'real' reading reduced stress levels more than having a cup of tea or listening to a piece of music. So eschew the listicle, the Instastory, the slideshow. Put down your phone and read a book made of paper. Slow reading is good for your health.

I dropped my laptop and it's fine. Reading is fine.

Sloth-Philosophy
Reading List

The sloth philosophy of books isn't just about reading slowly or reading something short, although both of these are fine. It's also about reading something that you enjoy and engage with just enough that you can forget about the world around you; or something that calms your anxiety or explains the world to you in a way that makes sense. Like these, hopefully:

THE SUMMER BOOK BY TOVE JANSSON

The Summer Book is about a girl and her granny (and occasionally a cat) who live together on a little island off the coast of mainland Finland during the summer. It's all about enjoying nature, learning what it means to love and living in the moment. Tove Jansson is best known for the *Moomintroll* children's series, but everyone should read her other books too and savour them. Jansson is a perfect author for the Slow Book enthusiast.

TO THE LIGHTHOUSE BY VIRGINIA WOOLF

This can be a challenging book to tackle, as it takes a while for your brain to adapt to its rhythm. Making the switch from reading listicles on your phone (The Top 7 Cities You Won't Believe Allow Pigs As Pets) to Woolf's languid prose can be kind of a shock. But this novel, about a family summering on Scotland's Isle of Skye, is a wonderful slow read.

THE LONG-LEGGED HOUSE BY WENDELL BERRY

This is a classic collection of nature writing from a writer who's been billed as a modern-day Thoreau. Kentucky-based author Berry is preoccupied with his place in the world – literally, with the homestead where he grew up. Equal parts philosophy, environmental activism and nostalgia, the essays are based on what it means to love of a piece of land; they're about feeling rooted to a place, what it means to return to it again and again and wanting to protect it from the dangers of modern life, whether that means development, pollution or simply the land changing hands. It's all about the slow, simple life – which makes for a great slow read.

THE LITTLE PRINCE
BY ANTOINE DE SAINT-EXUPÉRY

This sweet classic tale of figuring out one's place in the world is great to revisit when you're feeling stressed and in need of a bit of optimism in your life. The little prince travels the universe learning different life lessons about love and loss, until he ends up in the desert where he befriends a pilot. To give you a sense of the *Little Prince*'s massive appeal, the book has been in print since 1943 and has been translated into 300 languages. Probably because it's the ultimate slow read.

THE GUEST CAT BY TAKASHI HIRAIDE

Books about cats are always a smart choice for a slow read. *The Guest Cat* is all about a stray who begins visiting the house of a couple living in Tokyo and changes their lives for the better. Cats are fluffy balls of love and fur and they make great protagonists. Besides sloths, cats are probably the next-best example of how we should all be living our lives.

THE NEAPOLITAN NOVELS
BY ELEANA FERRANTE

Maybe 20 per cent of people who read these novels don't really get them and find them a bit slow or confusing (fair warning: there are a million characters to keep straight). For the remaining 80 per cent of people whose brains are calibrated properly, this series will be one of the most enthralling and rewarding reading experiences you'll ever have. The four-book series – the story of two girls growing up in Naples, Italy – explores love, friendship, romance, being female and learning to find your way in the world. The books are addictive. Try reading just one.

THE ALCHEMIST BY PAULO COELHO

This is the kind of book you read when you're 14 and it blows your mind and becomes your favourite book for a while (until you read *The Catcher in the Rye*). It's also fairly short. Originally published in Portuguese, it became an international bestseller. It's about a young shepherd who has a prophetic dream which takes him to Egypt to find some treasure; and it's about following your destiny. And those kinds of books are always nice.

ANY CHILDREN'S COLOURING BOOK

And who says slow reading has to actually involve reading? Because colouring books are technically still books, they're a great way to get your slow 'read' on – as long as you pick the right one. The billion-dollar adult colouring-book industry grew out of a need for harried adults to calm their anxiety in a quick and easy way. In reality, these books are extremely complex and stressful; just because we're grown up doesn't mean we're capable of filling in 300 tiny spaces on a butterfly's wing. Instead, buy a children's colouring book with nice, big, fat spaces and colour them in at your leisure. No more stressing out about how you didn't finish inking in the mitochondria from the magnified cell of the human body or the mermaid garden composed of a million plants.

Tulum or Palm Springs? Oslo or Berlin?
Let me just hug this globe while I decide.

Sloth Philosophy
Enjoy the journey

'A good traveller has no fixed plans and is not intent on arriving.'

Lao Tzu

Sloth Fact: Sloths have a massive online presence. They star in memes, viral videos, have blogs dedicated to their lives and (at the time of writing) over 100k Instagram #. But despite living the good life in places like beautiful Costa Rica and Panama, sloths aren't into documenting themselves online. You won't find any sloth selfies or vacation photos from these mammals who spend their entire lives unplugged. Whatever they do and wherever they travel it's for their own enjoyment, not anyone else's. Think they might have the right idea?

You may have heard about the negative effects of social media on travel. 'Instagram crowds may be ruining nature,' says National Public Radio in America, while a headline in the British newspaper the *Independent* despairs: 'How Social Media Ruined My Summer Holiday'. The issue is crowds of travellers descending on a destination for the sole purpose of proving online that *they were there* – a practice that is angering locals and wasting a depressing amount of our holiday time. On average, vacationers spend about nine hours on social media for every week of vacation, according to a study by online travel company Expedia. Ten per cent of respondents admitted to taking up to 15 selfies at a time to make sure they're getting the best holiday shot. And it isn't just our own faces we're posting to the interwebs – we're documenting everything wherever we go. A Santorini school had to post a sign asking snap-happy tourists to please refrain from taking photos of the pupils playing outside. We're obsessing over our online presence at the expense of living in the moment – especially now that most UK phone plans offer free data throughout Europe. It's difficult getting unplugged in this kind of atmosphere. But we must nevertheless do our best to try.

The sloth philosophy isn't about seeking out perfect alleyways, pleasing rock piles and cute blue doorways in order to view them through a lens and move on to get the next shot. It's a strange way to travel and it's also a bit dishonest. Why pretend you're the only person on the hill overlooking Machu Picchu when the place is crawling with other tourists getting the exact same picture? Travel is busy and messy and doesn't always go according to plan – and that's the beauty of it. The reason we travel is to get outside of ourselves and our lives for a bit. So enjoy ordering a flat white in German or a beer in Portuguese without immediately telling everyone about it. Take in the beauty of Antelope Canyon or Victoria Falls without needing to document it. Enjoy a street performer in Ankara playing accordion while his cat sings back-up vocals without needing to film it.* The sloth philosophy is about embracing the journey without needing a photo as a reward.

* You should film this. Use your common sense.

All the World's a Tree

*(after 'All the World's a Stage'
monologue in As You Like It by
William Shakespeare)*

All the world's a tree
And all the sloths merely sleeping;
They have their (excruciatingly slow) exits and
    their entrances,
And one sloth in his time plays very very few
    parts due to laziness,
His acts being minimal, except to eat and use
    the loo. At first, the infant,
slow, content in his mother's arms,
Then the languid little one, with his three-toed
    claws
And curious face, creeping like a snail
willingly to his nap branch. And then the
lover (just kidding. Sloths are too cute to
    make love). Then a soldier,

Full of excuses to explain his desertion (too
    much marching, too little napping),
Jealous in honour, slow and lumbering in
    quarrel,
Seeking not glory, but only the sun,
Even when the UV index is high. And then the
    justice,
In fair round belly with good tummy leaf-lined,
With eyes closed and fur of formal cut,
Full of bon mots and modern sleep practices;
And so he plays his part. The next age shifts
but looks like the ages before it, really,
Into the doddering sleep of the elder sloth,
With sloth spectacles on nose and
    grandsloths by his side;
His youthful exploits (none), his world just
    tree-wide
For his slowness is an expertise now, and he
    schools them,
When I was young, we knew how to be lazy.

And drifts off, mid speech. Last scene of all,
That ends this strange non-eventful history,
Is eternal childishness and blissful sloth
    oblivion,
Sans care, sans worry, sans rat race, sans
    everything.

Sloth Philosophy
Lean in to the science of relaxing music

Music is a great tool for helping us to relax. The right tune can help lower blood pressure, increase feelings of wellbeing and reduce stress. To achieve this effect, you'll want to choose songs on the slower side – not trap or grime or anything that makes you want to dance until 5 am. A UK study found the most relaxing music in the world is 'Weightless' by Manchester's Marconi Union. The eight-minute track beat contenders including Enya

Headphones nicely block out the squawking
of those damn macaws.

and Mozart, as the tune that clinically relaxed partic-ipants the most. With the soothing sounds of chimes, piano, guitar and some Buddhist chanting, 'Weight-less' proved scientifically more relaxing than a cup of tea or getting a massage! How does this work, exactly? A group of researchers in Malaysia found our heart-beats slow down to match the beat of the music – and the most relaxing type of music (resulting in increased relaxation and decreased stress in test subjects) was found to have around 60 beats per minute. So the next time you're stressed out, your heart pounding away, your thoughts racing, grab some headphones and find something with a slow tempo. Feel your heartbeat slow to match the rhythm of the music. Enjoy the sense of calm that comes from relaxing and slowing your heart rate to the beat of the sloth.

If you're looking for *live* music that embodies the philosophy of the sloth, however, check out 'As Slow as Possible', which is the longest and slowest piece of music in history. It's been playing on an organ in Germany since 2001.

Sloth Philosophy
Listening List

Musician Leonard Cohen lived in a monastery for something like ten years. He sat around, meditated and wrote poetry. When he was done with that, he returned to Los Angeles to plan a world tour at the age of 74. He played 247 shows on that tour. This is a classic sloth strategy: save up your energy – for a long time. And then do something fun when you feel like it.

'CLOSING TIME' BY LEONARD COHEN
While many Cohen songs follow the sloth philosophy this one is a particularly great starting point for sloth enthusiasts: 'Closing Time' is a beautiful acid trip of a song about staying out past your bedtime and enjoying the highs and lows of being alive (there's probably a deeper meaning to be found, but you get my drift).

SONATA K.448 BY MOZART

While the Mozart effect (the belief that listening to Mozart makes you smarter or helps you study better) is still not 100 per cent agreed on by scientists, there is definitive research proving that listening to the *Sonata K.448* reduces epileptic activity in the brains of sufferers. Music is amazing, right? This music can calm your brain and help you lean into that sloth life.

'CHEESEBURGER IN PARADISE'
BY JIMMY BUFFET

What song better encapsulates the sloth philosophy than this ode to comfort food and beach living?

'WHY DON'T WE GET DRUNK'
BY JIMMY BUFFET*

This is a song about getting drunk and having sex. Sloths don't drink, but if they did, they'd have slow, sensual sex while pleasantly drunk.

---

* Look – just listen to any Jimmy Buffet song. Unless the thought of margaritas, beaches and boats stresses you out for some reason.

'MARGARITAVILLE' BY JIMMY BUFFET

This is a song about enjoying life to the fullest by playing guitar, eating sponge cake and, of course, drinking margaritas.

'CAT'S IN THE CRADLE' BY HARRY CHAPIN

This is a song about a dad who was too busy to hang out with his kid until it was too late. Let this serve as a warning to you. Listen to the song, quit your job and take your kid to the zoo. Otherwise you'll be old and your kid won't visit you (except maybe over the holidays) because you were a bad parent.

'SAIL AWAY' BY ENYA

The Grammy-award-winning singer Enya lives in a remote castle in Ireland with her cats – at one time as many as twelve of them. This kitties-and-castle life-style is obviously relaxing and has led the world-famous singer to create some of the most chilled-out music you'll ever hear.

'DREAMS' BY GABRIELLE

This number-one hit in the UK is all about that feeling you get when you've finally found someone to love. There's also a line about not making any plans for tomorrow and living for tonight – classic sloth philosophy. Just enjoy the moment.

'SOMEONE LIKE YOU' BY ADELE

This is a bit of a downer in terms of subject matter – a woman lamenting that her lost love has found someone new – but Adele's voice can make anyone relax with a cup of tea or bottle of wine while reflecting on love and life. And that's what the sloth philosophy is all about: relaxing and reflecting.

'YELLOW' BY COLDPLAY

Inspired by the night sky in Wales, you'd be hard pressed to find a more chill song to put you to sleep. The band also admitted that the word yellow has no meaning whatsoever; it just sounded right in the song – and the sloth philosophy is all about some well-placed nonsense. This is great napping music.

Random Yet Practical Tips to Slothify Your Daily Life

1. Drive below the speed limit. Just for a few minutes. See how it feels. If your face feels hot and you've already been honked at a few times, that's excellent. Keep at it. It probably doesn't matter where you're going or when you get there. In the grand scheme of life, I mean. (Note: if you're late for a doctor's appointment this isn't the time to try this tip.)

2. Buy a pair of those fuzzy, shearling-lined shoes that double as slippers. Or perhaps they're slippers that double as shoes. There's no better feeling than going seamlessly from the house to the post office without having to bother with laces or buckles. Your lazy little feet will be so warm in those toasty sheepskin ovens, you'll never want to put on proper shoes again.

3. Remove one clock from your home. Time is arbitrary – modern time was invented by capitalists to standardise the work day, and we've all bought into it, which is a shame. Our lives are littered with digital and analogue clocks, reminding us with each tick that we're one second closer to the end. Revert to sloth time: sleeping when it seems like sleep time and otherwise eating a bit because you're hungry.

4. Do a bit of day drinking. There's nothing like a nice wine glow at 2 pm to put things into perspective. Resetting all your passwords because the Russians just hacked the entire internet and buying salad cream no longer seem so important, right? Just ease into that second glass of red and bask in the joy that comes from slowing down and enjoying life.

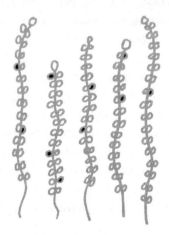

Is that your fur algae that smells so nice?

Love and Relationships

Whether it's a friendship or a relationship, our ability to give and receive love in a healthy way can have a big impact on happiness levels. Learning to live and love within the sloth philosophy will change your life.

Sloth Philosophy
It's all about enthusiasm

There's a reason why you're not sure what a sloth actually sounds like. That's because sloths are mostly silent creatures – until they're feeling sexy. Once the female has put her horniness out there into the forest universe, the male saunters over (slowly) to engage with her. Both parties get what they want and both leave satisfied (hopefully). The key takeaway here is this: the male sloth isn't going to bother a female that isn't ready or willing.

Let this be a lesson in consent for all those amorous would-be human lovers out there. The sloth philosophy is all about waiting until the moment is right and both parties are ready and willing. Because really, what's the hurry? Unless someone is dramatically and emphatically in the affirmative that they want to get intimate with you, move on. If they're in the mood, they will signal their readiness loud and clear – probably not by screaming, but perhaps with lots of smiling and nodding and positive language.

So next time you feel up for a bit of fun? Scream into the universe and wait for your prayers to be answered. Or save the yelling and do some online dating, which is probably a bit more practical.

Sloth Philosophy
Slow and sensual wins the race

'Sex is an emotion in motion.'

Mae West

Sloth Fact: Sloth sex is over in about five seconds.

We can learn a lot from the sloths, sexually. I know what you're thinking: five-second sex seems a bit of a waste. Why bother even getting undressed for that? And you'd be right. But the key here is that while male sloths ejaculate after five seconds, there is quite a bit of effort leading up to that. The sloth philosophy is about developing intimacy, romance and a cosmic connection with whoever it is that likes you back. The actual act of sex (while great) isn't the whole point. So learn from the sloths – take your time, have a bit of a chat and slowly get to know one another.

Quiz

What Kind of Sloth Lover Are You?

When it comes to dating your approach is:

A. meh – if I meet someone, I meet someone; maybe I'll find them at the second-hand vinyl store … or the bookstore

B. the universe will bring us together – I just need to be open, wear my love crystals every day and clear my flat of negative energy (also my dating profile features a yoga pose)

C. as many dates as possible in one night; it's pure statistics

What's your favourite sexy food?

A. Oysters

B. A tin of biscuits and a pack of string cheese

C. Papayas

Your ideal date would consist of:

A. the city centre for a show then a glass of wine at a nearby pub, followed by a tasteful naked photo shoot

B. origami class, followed by some mutual masturbation

C. hiking in the Andes followed by steamy sex in a tent

Answers

Mostly As: two-toed sloth. You're a traditional sort. Love happens when you're least expecting it, and when you find it, you want all the trappings associated with it – roses, chivalry, tender caresses and morning-after lie-ins. Being taken care of is always lovely. These romantic expectations might cause you to be a bit complacent in the bedroom, however. Remember, it is always better to give than receive (at least, 50 per cent of the time).

Mostly Bs: three-toed sloth. The more toes the better. You like to approach each sexual encounter with reverence, imagination and gratitude. Exploring and enjoying your partner is the height of sexiness for you. Whatever the situation, you respond with creativity and passion.

Mostly Cs: snake. A little unusual, a lot kinky. You love sex and everything about the physical act – and your partners love it too. But too much emphasis on the physical can mean you're neglecting the intellectual side of things. Try and increase the amount of intimacy with your partner, whether it's by having sex while you're both sober or spending more time together outside the bedroom.

I care about your well-being, little plant.

Sloth Philosophy
We all depend on
one another ...

Sloth Fact: Sloths and the tiny critters of the forest depend on one another. The sloth moth, for example, lives in the sloth's fur. They lay their eggs in sloth poo on the forest floor and when the larvae hatch they hitch a ride back up with the sloth and the cycle continues. Plus, after the moths die, the nutrients they leave behind feed a certain type of algae that flourish in the sloth's fur. Then the sloths eat the algae for a nutritious snack. It's a beautiful, furry ecosystem, right?

Get where I'm going with this? Embrace symbioses. We all have a purpose and we all depend on one another. The algae need the sloth and vice versa.

Someone else is probably depending on you too. Even if it's just your French bulldog. Or your employer. Or a plant.

The sloth philosophy acknowledges that we don't live in a vacuum and that we're all part of a grand ecosystem – friends, family, neighbours, loved ones and even strangers. We're all members of society and depend on everyone else within our community, honouring our shared social contract in order to function. We pay our taxes and the government provides schools and police and firefighters and doctors. We hold the door open for the person behind us and don't grope people on public transport or murder one another and generally act like respectful human beings when we're out and about – and others do the same for us. We all do this every day and so society functions properly. Accept that we all have a role to play. Thank your barista and hold the door open – the sloth (and the sloth moth) will thank you.

Sloth Philosophy
... but some kinds of dependencies are not so great

Sloth Fact: Sloths are wild animals and make terrible house pets. In fact, in many countries it's illegal for a private citizen to own one. Sloths do not like to be touched or groomed. They also require a specialised diet, a large outdoor space in which to roam and a hot, humid environment in order to thrive. Some animals are just better left to their own devices.

When you love something deeply and find it very adorable, your instinct is to own it, possess it, cage it, etc. You might even obsess over it. Want to track its movements and be with it all the time. This isn't always natural or best for both parties, however.

This kind of love can be destructive and lead to a lot of heartache. If someone doesn't want to be tamed by a relationship, or if they're offering up legitimate reasons as to why things aren't working for them, believe them. Many of us learn this the hard way. The sloth philosophy is all about allowing wild people their freedom – even when you really like or love them and want them to be tamed. You'll probably meet lots of these wild, free people who are busy pursuing their dreams (or doing too many pills or off travelling the world) and doing their own thing, but part of life is learning that those aren't the best people to plan a future around. It's nothing to do with you; they just aren't able to give you what you need.

The reasons for letting go of a wild someone you care about can be varied. But the fact is that some people, at certain points in their lives, are just better left to themselves. It's best to move on, forge ahead, find the next best thing that is perhaps more open to being domesticated. Like a cat. Or a nice person from your philosophy class.

There's Been an Incident at the Zoo

Sloth in a tree
Sloth in a tree

Hey, Mum, there's a sloth in a tree
He's still there
Can you see?

He's not doing much
He's sleeping and such

I expected more of a performance
Mum?
Make it see
I want it to do more
than just sleep in a tree

With this stick
Maybe
It will wake and look at me …
This sloth in a tree

Oh look!
It looks mad
And that makes me glad

What's that, Mum?
Bear enclosure next?
You're such a good mummy
to me

Sloth Philosophy
Practise deliberate solitude

'What is difficult?
To know oneself.'

Thales of Miletus

Sloth Fact: Sloths aren't social by nature and spend most of their time alone. You'll never be asked to join a sloth dinner party or to hit the pub with Suzy Two-Toed and her friends. Sloths just prefer to be alone. And we can all learn from that.

Solitude has a bit of a stigma these days. Cancelling plans to stay in, going by yourself to the theatre or fleeing to a cabin in the woods for a few

Alone with my brilliant thoughts.

months means you're having some kind of break-down (or assembling letter bombs while growing a beard). We're taught that spending time alone results in loneliness and isolation or that it encourages eccentricity. If we're alone, the thinking goes, we must be lacking love or happiness.

In actual fact, however, choosing to be alone has a number of psychological benefits. Deliberate solitude is a choice that can allow us to get some perspective, far from the maddening crowd. It encourages deeper thinking and creativity and improves concentration.

It's tough to do, though. We're used to constant stimulation from friends, our phones, our families … We don't really know how to be by ourselves. We're conditioned to want a partner, a relationship, someone to talk to. A study at the University of Virginia found that when participants were given the option of sitting alone at a table with no distractions or giving themselves an electric shock, a surprising number of them chose the shock. Researchers chalked up this instinct for self-harm to pure boredom. But are our own thoughts really so tedious? Have we lost the ability to be in our own company? With a bit of practice, we can all learn to enjoy the restorative, enriching and enlightening effects of solitude without feeling the need to shock ourselves to pass the time.

So try scheduling some time alone. Try and get a few minutes each day – whether it's a few minutes in the bathroom without your phone or a walk by yourself on your lunch break (or even a month at a bedsit by the sea, if you want to take it further than the day-to-day) – remember that seeking solitude is healthy. The sloth philosophy is about embracing the mental benefits of being alone (minus the phone).

The Flash Mob is Cancelled

There once was a sloth named Bob
He showed up two days late for his job
His fellow dancers didn't care
(they were sloths, they weren't there)
Dressed in spandex, Bob felt like a knob.

Winging an important speech in true sloth style.
Or maybe just yawning.

Work and School

Being a productive member of society, earning a living, getting good grades – the stress of accomplishing all these can make us feel a bit overwhelmed. What we can learn from the sloth about work and school is that sloths don't do either of them and have survived for millions of years.

'I'm lazy. But it's the lazy people who invented the wheel and the bicycle because they didn't like walking or carrying things.'

Lech Wałęsa

Sloth Philosophy
Reclaim the word lazy

'To do nothing at all is the most difficult thing in the world, the most difficult and the most intellectual.'

Oscar Wilde

Sloth Fact: Sloths aren't *lazy*. They're efficient. Sloths conserve energy by moving at a leisurely place, digesting food slowly and spending most of their time sleeping. They are very smart animals, but have the reputation for being the laziest species in the animal kingdom. Turns out, they're just victims of bad marketing. I mean, no one talks about a lazy clam. And it's not like they're out running marathons either.

Let's reclaim the word lazy, shall we? I'm not talking about commending the inability to become employed or keep a job or attend classes. I'm talking about celebrating the joyful laziness of lying on the couch with a takeaway in your hand and your phone on silent. The kind of laziness that lets your mind wander and your subconscious rise to the fore, allowing you to contemplate life and solve problems in a calm and measured manner. What looks like laziness is really efficiency; those on the move at all hours aren't necessarily better, despite what society wants us to think. We mistake a busy schedule for being important or smart or having more value. But science tells us otherwise.

Did you know 'thinkers' are lazier than non-thinkers? In other words, the smarter you are, the lazier you tend to be. How does that work? People with a high IQ don't need a lot of outside stimulation to be entertained. That means they can sit around, deep in thought, and be perfectly content, say, sitting and reading a book about hygge with a cup of coffee and a biscuit, while wearing a pair of socks, rather than racing around doing things for the sake of doing them. Some people require constant distraction, but it isn't the slothful among us. *Pick the kids up from school? Not likely. Too busy daydreaming about what my cat would look like in a tuxedo.* That's probably how companies like Tesla and Apple got started.

So next time you're getting home from a club at 5 am and see someone jogging down the street, just be content in the knowledge that you're probably a little bit smarter than them. Then head inside for a bit of sleep – you need to conserve energy for your next big world-changing project.

Sloth Philosophy
Be good at something and forget the rest

We've all heard the fable of the little duckling who fails the 100-metre dash in gym class. And she can't throw a ball, either. *What a pointless duckling*, her teachers think. *What is that duck even doing in school?* That is, until swimming class when the duck gets her own back. What a talented swimming duck! Who knew she had this secret skill when she was so bad at everything else?

The point of this fable is that no one is good at everything, but we're all good at something. We just

I'm very good at this.

need to determine what it is that we're good at and run (or crawl) with it. This can be hard in a world that respects certain skills over others. We value speed, ruthlessness, wealth and also the ability to code. But what if you're great at long conversations, making stew in the slow cooker and writing letters? What if you're a great girlfriend, but a shit marathoner? What if you're fab at baking bread, but bad at throwing a diamond hitch (old-timey Western reference). What if you're great chatting over coffee, but shit at emails?

It's very easy to beat ourselves up over the things we're not good at. And the pressure and guilt we may feel to improve at all costs must be avoided. You don't need to help yourself improve. You're probably fine just the way you are: perfect at some things and not so good at others. Join the club. In fact, forget that you don't understand cryptocurrency and instead make a list of things you're good at. I'll bet it's a pretty long one. So just embrace the sloth philosophy of being good at something – whatever that something is.

Famous Sloths

Oso Perezoso (Lazy Bear)

When little Oso the sloth decided to cross a busy highway in Ecuador he miscalculated: halfway across he gave up and was found clinging to the traffic barrier in the middle of the road. He shot to fame after photos of the police rescuing him went viral. Fans identified with the little guy's dilemma. Sometimes we all take on a bit more than we can handle – and a helping hand is always welcome.

Sloth Philosophy
Be still and chill

Sloth Fact: Sloths are the masters of motionlessness. They avoid predators by staying completely still. Making noise and moving around is the quickest way to get eaten by an eagle.

We're encouraged these days to lean in. Speak up. Have a voice. Make our opinions known. Engage, engage, engage! This is all well and good, but it can also help to know when to shut up, take a break and listen. It's OK to just exist in the world sometimes without seeking the spotlight – just watching, observing and learning. In fact, I'd argue that it's essential for your mental health.

The sloth philosophy of minding your own business is about acknowledging that it isn't your responsibility to speak your mind all the time and fight every battle. You don't even need to have an opinion on everything. (This isn't applicable in scenarios where people need your help or advice, by the way. You still need to be a nice person most of the time.)

Try and balance your need to get involved in every petty internet or family feud with the idea that maybe this is something you can sit out. Yes, your sister brought a similar pie (steak and ale – OK, exactly the same pie) to your mum's 75th birthday party. But *maybe* she forgot she was supposed to bring a Victoria sponge and wasn't just doing it to spite you. Let it go. By stepping back and not engaging you'll find peace.

It may help to think about this philosophy in terms of social media. The next time you want to fire off a witty retort or disagree with a former co-worker online, take a step back. Will entering the fray change anyone's mind about Brexit, or will it bring more shit and unpleasant feelings your way? Is this something you're mentally prepared to deal with or will it make you upset? If you feel your heart rate rising as you contemplate getting involved, it may be time to just be still and chill. You know what species is not at risk of extinction any time soon? Four out of six species of sloth. Let that be a lesson to you!

Sloth Philosophy
Identify the essential ...

'Nature does not hurry, yet everything is accomplished.'

Lao Tzu

Sloth Fact: Sloths don't have a lot of urgent action items on their agenda. Sleeping and eating are pretty much it. There is one essential task that they reluctantly address once or twice a month, however: using the loo (in their case, a hole in the forest floor).

Work and School

O ur world is full of urgent notifications – things we must complete by noon or the end of the day or week or month. We're under constant pressure and the looming threat of deadlines. But the fact is that there are very few things we actually *need* to do. Imagine explaining to your grandad about why you feel obliged to update your social-media feeds daily. He was a paratrooper in the war. He knows what's urgent and what isn't. Fighting fascists? Yes, good. Please get on with it. Posting a floppy-hat photo of you with your back to the camera in Positano? Not necessary.

Start the day with a to-do list, if lists are your kind of thing. Add the things you need to do to survive or help your children or pets survive. It probably looks something like: eat breakfast, feed cat, get dressed, eat lunch, go to school, drink water, etc. Focusing on the bare essentials is a great way to put things into perspective. Then all the other bullshit falls away. You don't need to buy new ankle socks. You don't need to reply to anyone's email. You don't *need* to make homemade baby food. They sell that in jars. The sloth philosophy is about acknowledging that sometimes focusing on the essentials is just fine.

Sloth Philosophy
... *then vow to do it later*

Sloth Fact: 'Why do anything today that you can put off until tomorrow?' is a sentiment attributed to humorist Mark Twain. The sloths embody this notion perfectly as they only use the toilet once every three weeks or so. Talk about needing a wee!

Procrastination, like laziness, is often misunderstood. *Just get on with it – you'll feel so much better,* cry the irritating, hallowed few who always meet their deadlines (preferably early). There's little regard for those who procrastinate naturally and who do best under the pressure of an imminent (or long past) deadline. Artists usually fall into this category. The 18th-century playwright Richard Sheridan famously turned in the final act for his play while the first two acts were being performed on opening night. The audience was none the wiser.

Those with impulsive tendencies also tend to be procrastinators. You know – that one friend who's always up for something? And you find yourself thinking, *Doesn't she ever have work to do?* She does. She's just putting it off, so she can spend time with you. Nice, right? A sunny day and a pint in the park are no match for her pending deadlines or a bathroom that needs cleaning. So remember, there's a method to this madness and just because procrastinators have a different timeline for getting things done doesn't mean theirs is the wrong way. So if you are well versed in the art of procrastination, rejoice. And if you're constantly stressed out by the need to meet deadlines and do everything all at once, try taking a step back. Remember the fourth tenet of the SLOW philosophy: 'What's the rush?'

There Once was a Sloth from Brisbane

His mum never gave him a name.
(She took her time to decide
Jerry, Joe, Horace, Clyde?)
Now a teen, this brings No Name great
    shame.

Sloth Philosophy
Take time to figure it out

'Slow down and enjoy life. It's not only the scenery you miss by going too fast – you also miss the sense of where you are going and why.'

Eddie Cantor, American entertainer

Sloth Fact: Sloths travel about 36 metres per day. That's a rate of about 2.5cm per minute. They don't care how long it takes to get anywhere. They're chill. So remember that slow and steady wins the race (if sloths were into racing, that is – which they're not).

Falling off the ladder is fine, too. You'll get there. Or you won't. You're still great!

Young people experience a lot of pressure to make up their minds about the future. What are you going to be when you grow up? What will you study at university? Where will you do an internship? What's the career path to your dream job? What's your start-up idea and where will you get funding? Are you on a hot-30-under-30 list yet? No? What's taking you so long to be successful, anyway? It's exhausting and stressful to feel that you owe anyone an explanation about your life or your career. The sloth philosophy believes in spending the time to figure it all out at your own pace – no matter how long that takes.

Take comfort in the idea that whether you're 14 or 45, if you don't know exactly what you're doing with your life, *it's OK* and you're in good company. Martha Stewart didn't publish her first book about entertaining until the age of 41 (before that she worked on Wall Street and owned a catering firm); Vera Wang opened her first bridal boutique at 41; Samuel L. Jackson was a stage actor until landing a starring role in *Pulp Fiction* at the age of 45; Ray Kroc was over 50 before he joined McDonald's; Laura

Ingalls Wilder was 65 when she published her first book, *Little House in the Big Woods*; artist Grandma Moses began painting in her 70s and wrote her memoir at 92; and the average age of an author on the *New York Times* bestseller list is 54. The point is that you've got plenty of time.

So when you're feeling overwhelmed or directionless, remember the SLOW method (*see page 5*) and ask yourself, 'What's the rush?' Many successful people didn't know what they wanted to be right after they graduated, so why should you? Part of life is about figuring it out as you go along, and there's no shame in that. Forget the idea that your education and career should be linear and accept that it's OK to drift, go in circles and change direction. It's all part of the journey.

Famous Sloths

Lola the Sloth

Lola found fame after appearing as a guest on *The Ellen Show* alongside actress Kristen Bell, who erupted in tears of joy and excitement when she saw Lola and the clip went viral. Lola now lives in California at the Wildlife Learning Center and has more than 16,000 social-media followers. You can buy a T-shirt with her face on it, if you need a reminder to 'hang in there', and she also makes appearances for 'educational' purposes. So if a sloth-themed birthday is on your bucket list, the staff at the learning centre can make that happen.

Let the light in. Even your naughty bits can
benefit from some vitamin D.

Beauty and Self-care

*Sloths are marvellously cute, despite being
extremely weird looking and having very poor
hygiene. The lesson of the sloth is about learning
to love and take care of ourselves in whatever way
happens to work for us.*

Sloth Philosophy
Do your own little dance

Sloth Fact: Before sloths poop, they do a little dance that involves a lot of butt wiggling. The lesson here is that rituals are important, and while you don't have to tap dance before having a wee, the sloth philosophy is all about embracing the self-care rituals that make life for you worth living – however weird they might seem to anyone else.

We spend a lot of time reading about how we should be and look and dress. But when we finally figure out what it is we like and embrace it – whether it's creating a personal style or vowing never to leave the house without mascara or spending a small fortune on a bottle of perfume or fancy haircut – we're often shamed for it. What extravagance! What vanity! What a waste of time! Then, when we *don't* welcome the latest trends, we're judged as being out of touch or backward. *Oh, the poop dance? That's so 2017 – it's all about flossing now!* The sloth philosophy embraces the little things that make you feel happy and look good, society be damned.

Hair masks, collagen capsules, lactic-acid serums, bronzing lotions, a tin of biscuits, fluffy slippers, black nail varnish – your own rituals can take many forms. The average beauty routine today is 27 steps long and takes about 40 minutes. (For those of us who grew up in the 90s, much of this time is now spent filling in over-plucked brows with tints and gels. Bushy brows are back, but we just look eternally surprised.) And what of it? Take whatever time you need to do whatever it is that you want. You're worth it. And you look fabulous.

Sloth Philosophy
But it's also OK to just let go

Sloth Fact: Sloths move so slowly that algae grow on them. It helps them to blend in with their surroundings. Their fur is also packed with beetles, bacteria, moths and fungus. But guess what? They're still lovely animals, no matter how much they 'let themselves go', according to society's arbitrary standards. Same goes for you.

Sometimes self-care means opting out of the selfie game for a while and not presenting your best self to the world. (Unless, of course, you want to post a #nomakeupselfie. Knock yourself out.) The sloth philosophy is all about slowing down your routines, taking a step back and allowing yourself the opportunity to do whatever you feel like.

Some days, whether it's because you're ill, depressed, overwhelmed or simply feeling lazy or hung over, just doing the bare minimum feels like a lot. Showering isn't the first thing you want to tackle, let alone moisturising your cuticles or having a healthy breakfast. But self-care also includes ordering fried chicken in bed and not shaving your armpits for a few days, if that's what you feel like doing. Sometimes our brains and bodies need a break. Or some medication. Or some therapy. It's your life – you know what's best for you. So don't be afraid to do the absolute bare minimum for a bit. Lounge. Embrace the greasy hair. Let the algae grow! Just exist as a person without being productive or getting things done. The sloth philosophy is all about giving yourself a break from all those expectations.

Slothify your Wardrobe

The sloth philosophy is all about looking good and being comfortable without expending a lot of effort. Sloths have fur, which gives them an advantage over us, of course: fur is much more comfortable (and adorable) than the dry, itchy skin sacks we've been blessed with. Nevertheless, we can maximise the sloth potential of our wardrobes quite easily with a few simple steps.

1. Embrace stretchy fabrics that keep their shape and don't need to be ironed. While ironing is actually a nice, slow activity that can focus the mind, it's also kind of a pain. Better to embrace materials that don't bag at the knees after one wear.

2. Avoid constricting clothing. Forget the waist trainer or the high-waisted jeans. Yes, they keep your tummy in, but as soon as you sit down the denim squeezes all your rolls and makes you want to throw up. They make lovely, soft, stretchy denim for a reason.

3. The washing machine is your friend. Dry clean only is an exercise in sadomasochism.

4. Splurge on some high-quality loungewear. Buy that matching velour tracksuit you've had your eye on. Get those fluffy wool-lined slippers. Being able to relax and be comfortable (while looking fab) brings you one step closer to slothful bliss.

My fur is a 24/7 tracksuit. Jealous?

Sloth Philosophy
Sloth love is self-love

Everyone is unique. That's just part of being human and it's cause for celebration. We are taught this at a young age and then, as we grow up, we get bullied mercilessly in school for being a bit weird – then we realise being different is hard and maybe not so desirable, after all. The pressure to conform, even as an adult, is real. Suddenly, going bra-less with tiny boobs is trending and big-boobed women are left feeling inadequate. High-waisted jeans are in fashion, but are also kind of uncomfortable for those of us with a muffin top. And there's always the latest in trendy hair colouring that costs a fortune to maintain. The sloth philosophy is about unlearning our fear of standing out thanks to years at school with a bunch of mean little sociopaths.

So whether it's your brain or your body that's a bit different from everyone else's, the way of the sloth demands that you acknowledge and accept your otherness. If your nips are up in your pits or you've got a funny left toe, embrace whatever makes you special and unique. That goes for your personality, too. Extrovert or introvert, loud and dancing on the tables or quiet and passed out quietly in the club, we've all got something to offer. And knowing that truth will bring you one step closer to the wisdom of the sloth.

Live Slow, Die Whenever

Ode to Living Slow and Dying Whenever
Oh withered desk souls
Oh sad business lunch
Oh working for the weekend
For vacation
For retirement
Oh shiny bank machines
Shiny black shoes
Shiny watches paid for with shiny coins
Shiny faces slathered with expensive creams
Join us!
Take to the trees!
Take off your ties!
(You can't tie them with just three claws
    anyway)
Take a nap!
At three pm or at midnight!
Take time

To wander
Take a month
To eat a meal
Slow slung from branch to branch
Let your shoes drop to the forest floor
Let your hair down
Let the sun work magic
Slow deliverance from alarms and sirens and
    schedules
Trust us
the sloths
We're ready for you
Join us

Sloth Philosophy
Hang on to your stuff with a death grip

'If life must not be taken too seriously, then so neither must death.'

Samuel Butler, British author

Sloth Fact: Sloths are too lazy to even fall out of a tree when they die. A sloth's grip is so strong it remains clinging to its branch after passing away. Remember that on your next trip to Costa Rica. That cute sloth you snapped snoozing away up there? It might well be dead.

We have a lot to learn from how sloths pass away. They die in a place they love and cherish (a tree), clinging to the thing they probably love most (a branch). What more could we hope for when it comes time for our own passing?

There's a movement afoot now, however, that encourages us to 'declutter' everything we care about and organise our lives in preparation for death. *The Swedish Art of Death Cleaning* by Margareta Magnusson is the latest in the trend of Scandinavian books telling us to how to be. Too stressed? Buy a candle. Unhappy? Live like a Dane. Near death? Clean out your house. While this may work for some people, the sloth philosophy is about approaching the end of your life with a bit of self-kindness and a light touch. You've made it this far, the sloth thinking goes, so why start suddenly worrying about purging it all for the sake of the kids or grandkids who might not want to deal with it? The things you accumulate over a lifetime are filled with memories and meaning – and that's OK. Dried flowers from your wedding-vow renewal, campaign button for the re-election of Dennis Skinner, a bottle of your mother's perfume, an old KitKat. Keep it all. (Or you can eat the KitKat, actually.)

In Conclusion: Life is Short – Spend it Doing Things You Love

'I am happiest when I am idle. I could live for months without performing any kind of labour, and at the expiration of that time I should feel fresh and vigorous enough to go right on in the same way for numerous more months.'

Artemus Ward, American humorist

Sloth Fact: Depending on the species, sloths can live anywhere from 20 to 30 years of age, and up to 40 years in captivity.

In conclusion, none of us is guaranteed a set amount of time on this earth. Really, it's a miracle we are here at all. In 17th-century England the average life expectancy was just 35. If you survived childbirth, you could expect to perish from disease or overwork or a gruesome accident. Today we've got it a bit better but, of course, it's all up to chance and luck – we never know what's in store for us. So take a leaf from the sloth tree of life and make the most of your time on earth. Spend it doing the things you love – sleeping, hanging out, bringing joy to others.* Whatever you want! It's your life.

---

* Or eating. The sloth philosophy understands that ice cream helps you live life to the fullest.

You did it. You read the entire thing. Or you skimmed it. Either way, we're proud of you.

HarperCollinsPublishers
1 London Bridge Street
London SE1 9GF

www.harpercollins.co.uk

First published by HarperCollins*Publishers* 2018

9 10 8

Text and poetry © Jennifer McCartney 2018
Illustrations © Clare Faulkner 2018
All poetry is the author's own unless otherwise stated

Quote on page 41 reprinted by permission of
HarperCollins*Publishers* Ltd © 1977, Agatha Christie

Jennifer McCartney asserts the moral right to
be identified as the author of this work

A catalogue record of this book is
available from the British Library

HB ISBN 978-0-00-830482-9
EB ISBN 978-0-00-830483-6

Printed and bound in Great Britain by
CPI Group (UK) Ltd, Croydon, CR0 4YY

MIX
Paper from
responsible sources

FSC www.fsc.org **FSC® C007454**

This book is produced from independently certified FSC paper
to ensure responsible forest management.

For more information visit: www.harpercollins.co.uk/green